Routledge Revivals

Sisyphus

First published in 1929, *Sisyphus* offers a compelling examination of psychology's potential and limitations as a "young" science. Jaeger explores its profound impact on understanding human behavior and shaping society, while critically addressing its boundaries. Praised for its "acumen and knowledge" by the Manchester Guardian, this concise work remains essential reading for those interested in psychology, philosophy, and the history of science.

Sisyphus

Or the Limits of Psychology

M. Jaeger

Routledge
Taylor & Francis Group
ROUTLEDGE REVIVALS

First published in 1929
by Kegan Paul, Trench, Trubner & Co., Ltd.

This edition first published in 2026 by Routledge
4 Park Square, Milton Park, Abingdon, Oxon, OX14 4RN

and by Routledge
605 Third Avenue, New York, NY 10158

Routledge is an imprint of the Taylor & Francis Group, an informa business

Publisher's Note
The publisher has gone to great lengths to ensure the quality of this reprint but points out that some imperfections in the original copies may be apparent.

Disclaimer
The publisher has made every effort to trace copyright holders and welcomes correspondence from those they have been unable to contact.

For Product Safety Concerns and Information please contact our EU representative GPSR@taylorandfrancis.com. Taylor & Francis Verlag GmbH, Kaufingerstraße 24, 80331 München, Germany

A Library of Congress record exists under LCCN: 30009521

ISBN: 978-1-041-33767-6 (hbk)
ISBN: 978-1-003-78947-5 (ebk)
ISBN: 978-1-041-33768-3 (pbk)

Book DOI 10.4324/9781003789475

SISYPHUS

OR

THE LIMITS OF PSYCHOLOGY

BY

M. JAEGER

Author of "The Question Mark," "The Man with Six Senses," etc

LONDON

KEGAN PAUL, TRENCH, TRUBNER & CO., LTD.

NEW YORK: E. P. DUTTON & CO.

1929

PRINTED IN GREAT BRITAIN BY MACKAYS LTD., CHATHAM

SISYPHUS

OR

THE LIMITS OF PSYCHOLOGY

I

In the classical tradition of the "To-day and To-morrow" series did not exercise gentle pressure on the choice of comparisons, it might seem ungracious to liken the labour of our modern psychologists to those of Sisyphus, when they might be more aptly compared to those of a much more up-to-date (and how much more successful!) hero.

"The Baron, once, when he was in England, performed a much more extraordinary feat of strength, as I shall now relate to you.

"He wished one day to leap on his wonderful horse over a very wide and deep pond. I represented to him that it was not possible to make this leap; but when he has made up his mind, it is impossible to prevail on him to change it, as you all well know. He persisted in his resolution and made the leap. . . . and fell into the pond up to his neck! I thought he and his steed were lost, for the pool was evidently very deep, when, to my astonishment, he took hold of his queue of hair, and actually lifted himself out of the pool with his horse under him, by the mere pressure of his knees.

"This anecdote made a great impression on his hearers."

No doubt it did. Yet a child who is most willing to believe in all the great Baron's other adventures—who finds no difficulty at all with the eight-legged hare, or the cloak with hydrophobia, is apt to become a little uneasy over this particular incident. In the same way, the ordinary intelligent adult, who tries, at due distance, to follow the movements of modern scientific thought, who thinks he gets fitful, fascinating glimpses of the sort of thing that Einstein may mean, and still hopes that someone may some day make the Theory of Quanta intelligible, occasionally feels a similar uneasiness over the claims of modern psychologists.

This uneasiness is perhaps worth analysis, if only in order that the experts may set about dispelling it. There is good reason why they should do so, in that psychology is important not only to the expert but to the ordinary person. Relativity and the constitution of the atom have, after all, little direct bearing on every-day conduct; but there are people (few yet in England, many more in the United States) who are directing their lives—and the lives of others—according to the doctrines of Freud or Watson; or even sometimes by a queerly incongruous mixture of the two.

At the root of the sceptical layman's difficulty is the essential difference between psychology and all the other sciences; the fact that it is an attempt to study the instrument of study itself—the human mind. For this reason, those assumptions unobtrusively made in all other branches of investigation, and never brought into question—such assumptions as the existence of objective truth, the validity of human reason, the possibility of complete intellectual detachment in the observer—themselves become matters for investigation in any comprehensive psychological system. And yet no progress, no beginning even, is possible, unless these assumptions are already granted — Münchausen has only his own hair to lay hold on. If, for instance, we are of opinion that two and two make four only because it is biologically desirable that they should, we shall not find it easy to prove even our theory itself—that reason assents to what is biologically desirable—or, for that matter, to prove anything whatever.

This root difficulty seems to give a paradoxical quality to the whole structure of modern psychology, so that one is apt to find psychologists inadvertently assuming what is to be proved or even occasionally of assuming what they suppose themselves to be disproving. And practical applications of Freudian and Behaviorist theory naturally show corresponding signs of trouble, often humorous, but not the less disquieting when one considers that they may be energetically applied to all of us, as already to some, if the less sane of our theorists ever get out of hand.

It is the object of this essay to bring together a few of these fallacies in theory and discords in application in the hope of finding some useful indication as to what modern psychology can do for us and (no less important) what it cannot.

THE LIMITS OF PSYCHOLOGY

II

MAY one assume one's own mind to be completely healthy and therefore a competent judge in the matter when the whole question is what constitutes healthy-mindedness?

Freud and his disciples have no doubt about their conception of healthy-mindedness. It is the completest possible degree of consciousness, involving (as Freud himself puts it in his latest book, *The Future of an Illusion,*) "the primacy of the intelligence." For him, the ideal is that man shall know to the highest possible extent what he is about, so that he may no longer be at the mercy of those instincts and unconscious impulses on whose power the psycho-analysts have themselves laid so much stress. *The Future of an Illusion* is a pæan (and, probably the strongest anti-Freudian will admit, a fine one) to the intellect; that is, to that human faculty in which the writer himself excels. He prophesies its triumph:

> "We may insist as much as we like that the human intellect is weak in comparison with human instincts and be right in so doing. But, nevertheless, there is something peculiar about this weakness. The voice of the intellect is a soft one, but it does not rest until it has gained a hearing. Ultimately, after endlessly repeated rebuffs, it succeeds."

However strongly one may sympathize with these views and aspirations, it is important to remember that they are no more than views and aspirations, not verifiable in the same sense as the existence of the planet Neptune was verifiable, for instance. Other conflicting ideals remain possible and there is no outside standard by which to judge among them. The writer implicitly makes the claim, made *ipso facto* by all psychologists who push on into the region of morals, "my mind is the standard of mental health."

Though *The Future of an Illusion* is a criticism of the religious instinct, yet the author admits the psychological value of religious faith :

> "The true believer," he says, "is in a high degree protected against the danger of certain neurotic afflictions; by accepting the universal neurosis, he is spared the task of forming a personal neurosis."

But if this is admitted, there may be matters in which the believer will be a sounder guide than the agnostic—even perhaps in this very question of the standard of mental health.

The strength of the psycho-analytic gospel lay in its origin as a practical method of dealing with certain nervous aberrations; its weakness appears when it tries to develop into scientific theory. Our working standard with regard to mental eccentricities has always hitherto been that of social convenience. It is as arbitrary as our judicial code. We send a man to a mental specialist or, in the last resort, to an asylum, when he has become intolerable to his neighbours. Suppose a change in social conditions by which a type of mental development which is now found intolerable became innocuous, or even advantageous, would there be any valid reason why our psychiatrists should not cease trying to cure such cases, should not even encourage them? It is one thing to say that we will get rid of one kind of mentality because, under existing conditions, we find it unendurably tiresome, and quite another to say that this or that type of mind is in itself wholesome or unwholesome. Primitive types are regarded as insane when they appear among us now; on the other hand, it seems likely that the average Londoner would have been counted at least mentally deficient if he had appeared in ancient Athens. If, in the same way, a man of the future has ever been born into this twentieth century of ours, he may very well be in Earlswood, if not in Broadmoor. Even in our own experience, at the same period when it was a crime to leave one's curtains undrawn at night, men were psychologically treated because they could not live under conditions of danger, noise and filth such as would never have arisen in their every-day existence.

In this immediate practical business of making the exceptional man at least temporarily able to endure his environment, there is no doubt that psycho-analysis has had its successes. Even in this limited sphere, however, the lay observer cannot escape the impression that it is still very much a hit or miss affair. Its own advocates often regard it as a last resort, "more risky than a major operation." There are obvious reasons for this, even if the assumptions on which the method is based are granted, in that the man who applies it is himself no more than a man and subject to the same kind of influences as the mind he is investigating. It is hardly necessary at this time of day to quote instances of the psycho-analyst who reads his own 'complexes' into his patients. Opportunities to say "Physician, heal thyself," are so abundant that it would be almost ungenerous to take advantage of them if the matter were not one of practical importance. When one finds a psycho-analytic practitioner who makes his wife unhappy by chronic inability to be polite to her friends, one cannot help wondering whether the cures claimed by him were not rather a matter of good luck than good management.

If one plays at random with a tangle of string, it sometimes straightens itself out. If a child is bored or worried to the limit by its elders, there sometimes results a nerve storm in which the naughtiness is blown away in the general cataclysm. The adult who cannot remember some such occasion in his or her own childhood must have been uncommonly fortunate. At a later stage, the school child learns to assent to anything in the 'for-goodness-sake-let's-get-it-over' spirit. "Of course, I cried and said I was sorry," says the irrepressible schoolgirl. "I knew I shouldn't get away until I did."

Here is a description by Freud of 'transference' in his treatment of grown-up children:

> " At least once in the course of every analysis a moment comes when the

patient obstinately maintains that just now positively nothing whatever occurs to his mind. His free associations come to a stop and the usual incentives for putting them in motion fail in their effect. As a result of pressure the patient is at last induced to admit that he is thinking of the view from the consulting-room window, of the wall-paper that he sees before him, or of the gas-lamp hanging from the ceiling. Then one knows at once that he has gone off into the transference and that he is engaged upon what are still unconscious thoughts relating to the physician; and one sees the stoppage in the patient's associations disappear as soon as he has been given this explanation.'"[1]

Certainly, such an explanation might be expected to start a very active train of thought.

In spite of such excursions into comedy, however, the prestige acquired by the psycho-analytic technique must

[1] *Group Psychology and the Analysis of the Ego.*

have something to justify it. But statistics are badly needed. In the works of Freud and other writers, one reads of treatments that have been brought to a successful conclusion; in newspapers one reads occasionally of those that have ended in the suicide of the patient. But there has not yet been, so far as I can discover, any systematic investigation by an impartial authority into an unselected group of cases, stating how many succeeded, how many failed, and how many had inconclusive results.

Such a tabulated record would be practically valuable. It would also lead back once more to the root theoretic difficulty of the question, in that there would, in some cases, be differences of opinion as to what constituted success. It is a standing joke that the patient frequently dies after a completely successful operation. To some tastes, several English poets have died (as poets) after a plunge into psycho-analysis. Here again, we meet with the assumption that we already know what we want of the human mind. Whereas we know only, and that very roughly and uncertainly, what we do not want. As to what we ought to want—will such knowledge ever be possible? We need some god to tell us that.

There is a well-authenticated story of a group of nerve specialists who tried out a new psychiatric device upon themselves. It consisted of a variety of the word sequence, so familiar to the readers of modern detective fiction. A string of words, some of more emotional significance than others, is read out to the subject. He responds with the first word suggested to him in each case, and his mental condition is indicated by the nature of the response, its promptness or tardiness, sometimes also by measurements of his blood pressure and other physical changes.

In this instance, to the dismay of his colleagues, the most eminent gentleman present gave all the 'imbecile reactions.'

One trusts that this particular bit of mechanism was returned to the manufacturer as defective. But how about the mechanisms that get through and are adopted? They may allow mental specialists to pass with honours. Will they necessarily, therefore, pass the most valuable human beings? Would Confucius, or St Francis, or Dr Johnson, or Darwin be perfectly safe with them? Can they be guaranteed not to cure Blake of visions, or Leonardo da Vinci of mental restlessness? The problem is not so remote as it sounds. If we are not careful, we may actually be getting our potential Blakes and Leonardos cured while they are too young to resist; for many teachers are by this time enthusiastic psycho-analysts.

SISYPHUS

The ideal human being has varied considerably throughout the ages, and there are those to whom this latest one of fully self-conscious man appeals even less than that (for instance) of the pack leader, or the religious ascetic, or the epicurean. Nor can it be said that the examples shown by followers of the new cult are always enticing—though it would probably be doing Freud (who is, at the lowest and most hostile estimate, a man of thought and culture) and his saner followers a gross injustice to suppose that they would be anything but horrified—one might say 'shocked,' if the word in this connection did not seem almost a blasphemy—by some of the attempts at present made towards the attainment of their ideal.

An oppressive air of frankness for its own sake overhangs the haunts of such futurists in the art of living. Everyone watches everyone else in the hope of detecting repressions, while seizing every chance to show that he, at least, has none. Faintly one hears inhibited modesty crying for release; pent-up reticence struggles vainly for an outlet; sternly repressed Puritanism finds odd, twisted channels of escape. In such circles, a woman hardly dare refuse to smoke, however much she may dislike the process. Skirts worn below the knee are almost an occasion for the ostracism of the culprit. You must run down your parents to show that you are free of the incest complexes; it is bad manners and worse if you have not a stock of such stories as were once confined to the commercial rooms of provincial hotels.

And when all is done, it is to no purpose, for no one really believes in your free uninhibited consciousness. Such belief would be itself against the code. One devotee was heard to say recently that she never now accepted any remark made to her at its face value. Mercifully, one need not accept this remark, at least, at its face value, for, of all the inhibitions, this would surely be the most terrible. Happier far the innocent who believes implicitly everything that he is told! But it is true that in conversation with real initiates one has an odd dizzy sensation that words are changing their value almost momentarily like marks at the time of the slump.

Perhaps all these are no more than necessary, though unprepossessing, experiments on the road to fully self-conscious man. Yet it may be found that even the finished product, when he appears, will prefer to keep one small department of the soul which he does not attempt to explain completely even to himself. Socrates, with his motto "Know thyself," is sometimes claimed as their prototype by the psycho-analytic school. But Socrates also confessed that all he knew was that he knew nothing and relied upon a 'daimon' to make his decisions for him at moments of crisis. And the 'daimon' (apt to be uncomfortably ignored by the philosopher's modern admirers) was perhaps, after all, the strongest evidence of Socrates' wisdom. Like Saint Joan's voices (if one accepts Bernard Shaw's interpretation) it told him to do what he chose to do, making it unnecessary to explain why. And after all, has Freud himself any better reason for his faith in the 'primacy of the intelligence'?

SISYPHUS

III

"For Heaven's sake, let us stick to what we can see! " So, in unscientific language, one might render Dr Watson's attitude towards the cloudy, shifting, complicated structures built up by less practical psychologists.

Accordingly, he confines himself to the study of human behaviour as it can be observed from outside and to the conclusions that can be drawn from those observations.

"We must study the simple and complex things which call out action in man; how early in life he can react to the various simple and complex sense stimuli; at what age he usually puts on the various instincts, and what the situations are which call them out. Just what is the pattern of his instinctive acts—that is, does the human being, apart from training, do any complex acts instinctively as do the lower animals? If so, what is man's full equipment of instincts? When does emotional activity manifest itself? And what are the situations which call it out? And what special acts can be observed in emotional behaviour? How soon can we observe the beginning of habits in infants? What special methods can we develop for rapidly and surely implanting and retaining the body and speech habits which society demands?'"[1]

His work on these lines has led Watson to the view that all human behaviour can be expressed in terms of stimulus and reaction. He sees the human being as a penny-in-the-slot machine. You put in your coin and are

[1] *Psychology from the Standpoint of a Behaviorist.*

presented with a piece of chocolate. Or, if you are not, that can only be because there is something wrong with the works. Of course, the human mechanism is more complicated than this, but the principle is the same. Watson invites his students to regard man as "an assembled organic machine ready to run."

As to what a man finds, or thinks he finds, in his own mind, in looking inwards, all this should, in the Behaviorist's view, be ignored as unverifiable. Of such terms as 'sensation,' 'perception,' 'attention,' 'will,' 'image,' and the like, Watson confesses frankly: "I do not know what they mean, nor do I believe that anyone else can use them consistently."[1] When a man expresses such notions in words, that is merely one more verbal reaction to be studied. It follows, of course, that the investigator cannot

[1] *Psychology from the Standpoint of a Behaviorist.*

claim any other value for his own introspections.

It is a refreshing point of view and fruitful. No scientist could quarrel with its methods, which have brought interesting results and will certainly bring more. Whether this science can properly be called ' Psychology,' or anything but the sufficiently descriptive term ' the science of Behaviour,' is another question. It seems rather a new liaison science between Physiology and Psychology. Dr Watson's quarrel with more orthodox psychologists lies in his claim that it is the whole of Psychology—in other words, capable of explaining human nature completely.

From the first, however, the Behaviorists have been crippled in their investigations, and the hindrance is not scientifically irrelevant. It consists in a sentiment against experiments on human beings; and since this sentiment itself is a part of human behaviour, and human behaviour cannot be effectually controlled until many of these experiments have already yielded their results, it looks as if the infant science were to be from the start involved in a vicious circle.

Uncontrolled observation can, of course, contribute something, and mild and simple experiments can be, and have been, carried out, where parents are willing to hazard their offspring in the interests of science, or where the babies are in the charge of orphanages and other institutions. Up to the present, such experiments seem to have been chiefly confined to such minor discourtesies as twitching a blanket from under a sleeping infant in order to show his 'fear reaction to loss of support.' On one occasion Dr Watson was even permitted to 'build in' a fear reaction to furry animals into an eleven-months baby, Albert B., by hammering a steel bar whenever a white rat appeared, so that ultimately the mere sight of the creature produced shrinking and tears. But the experimenter aims at a much more comprehensive study:

"In order to get a picture of his emotional behaviour, we have to test separation from mother. We have to test him with different and uncustomary foods, with strange people to feed him, with strange nurses to bathe him, clothe him and put him to bed. We must rob him of his toys, of things he is playing with. We must let a bigger boy or girl bully him, we must put him in high places, on ledges (making injuries impossible, however), on the backs of ponies or dogs."[1]

The first emotional reaction of the ordinary person to such proposals is apt to be one of disgust and indignation. But the matter cannot be

[1] *Behaviorism.*

dismissed quite so simply as that. The experiment on Albert, and others like it, for instance, suggested how fear reactions already established in children might be removed. The furry animals were accompanied by food instead of by loud noises, and, with a little time and patience, the child would play with them with one hand while it ate with the other. Such an instrument for mitigating the tortures suffered by nervous children might, by some, be considered cheap at the price of a little distress cautiously inflicted on a few. On the other hand, the perils of such a concession are obvious enough.

This question of psychological experiment on human beings is clearly going to be one of the problems of the immediate future, and will involve similar arguments to those used for and against Vivisection. In this case, however, the triumph of Science seems less assured. If Watson's view of man as an organic machine were already generally accepted with all its implications, probably antagonism to experiments on that pretentious puppet would be greatly reduced. But then, again, the experiments are needed to prove the theory.

It may be conjectured that such experimentation will be allowed to go further in the United States or, at least, in some of them, than in Europe. Watson's work began there, and patriotism is certainly one of the factors in the great prestige his doctrines have won on that side of the Atlantic, while on this side they are still almost unknown to the ordinary cultured person. Moreover, without committing oneself to the view that there is less sentiment and aesthetic fastidiousness, or more scientific curiosity, in the United States than in Europe, one may perhaps safely say that these things exist there more in isolation. The elements of civilization and culture seem to be less completely fused in that vast and varied country where Ku Klux Klan horrors flourish beside Leagues of Universal Brotherhood, and unexampled prosperity is compatible with unemployment figures of four million. If teachers of evolution are persecuted at one end of the country, sterilization of the unfit is practised at the other. Where the right hand realizes so little what the left hand is doing, practical possibilities in all directions are enlarged to a degree almost alarming to the more squeamish European.

What, however, remains a moral certainty is that psychological experiment will never anywhere be allowed to go as far as the scientists would like. For Dr Watson's purposes, for instance, extensive experiment on subjects at the period of adolescence would obviously be of the highest importance, while, at the same time, presenting difficulties far greater than those on infants, and perhaps insuperable. The theory is thus apparently doomed to remain an hypothesis with very limited means of verification, and one can only speculate on the outcome if Watson and his disciples were able to carry their investigations methodically forward into the more subtle phases of adult mental life.

Macdougall twitted the new psychology with claiming its triumphs chiefly in the nursery, a criticism which seems a little unfair in view of its peculiar difficulties. Still, these limitations have certainly enabled the Behaviorists to evade, or skim over, many complicated problems of Psychology. If they had been content to leave them alone, altogether, with an admission of ignorance, their position would have been invulnerable. Sisyphus would have paused at a safe point and could have surveyed in triumph the extended view he had already attained. But no more than any of his rivals has Dr Watson been able to resist the fatal hill-top looming ahead, this desire of man to understand his own being completely.

Watson covers the phenomenon of thought only at the expense of deserting his original standard of direct observation. When a man produces complex results after a period of apparent quiescence, it is obvious that something must have happened in the meantime. The ingenious behaviorist explanation is that the man has in fact been behaving vigorously (though invisibly) during the whole interval; he has been talking to himself with all his energy, only his speech has been sub-vocal. It has consisted in abortive movements of the larynx, lips and tongue, repressed, as he was long ago trained to repress them when his childish meditations disturbed grown-up companions. If some drug paralysed all the muscles in question, he would presumably no more be capable of a complicated train of thought than the ordinary person can multiply 952 by 647 without pencil and paper. The more elementary forms of thought—the shrug, the raised eyebrow, the clenched fist and so on—would remain possible, as also emotional response (' the behaviour of the gut ') much of which has never been ' verbalized '—that is, in the more familiar Freudian diction, "become conscious."

No one can say that this is not so; though Dr Watson's description of the rat-in-the-maze behaviour of the man told to think out a problem aloud—clumsily trying one thing after another until he hits the right one—does not seem to prove anything conclusive. It might, in fact, merely mean that reflection is hampered by the presence and demands of an investigator.

Köhler found even his apes capable of using a stick to pull in a banana without haphazard efforts. Incidentally, as Bertrand Russell has pointed out, the rats in these cases behave uncommonly like Americans, and the apes strangely like Teutons.

But if no one can say certainly that Watson's account of the nature of thought is incorrect, no one can prove that it is the correct one. Nor is it conceivable that even the most delicate instruments for measuring laryngeal movement will ever be able to prove it. At this point Watson's theory becomes as purely speculative as any of those which he began by denouncing.

To the Behaviorist, human personality is thus nothing more than a network of acquired habits. Human beings, apart from physical inadequacies, are born equal. Genius comes down to "the formation of early work habits in youth, of working longer hours than others, of practising more intensively than others "[1]—a definition strangely unsatisfactory to anyone who has had to do with one of those exasperating beings who can do so much more than anyone else with so much less trouble. But Dr Watson thinks he could create genius:

"The behaviorists believe that there is nothing from within to develop. If you start with a healthy body, the right number of fingers and toes, eyes, and the few elementary movements that are present at birth, you do not need anything else in the way of raw material to make a man, be that man a genius, a cultured gentleman, a rowdy, or a thug."[2]

It is an awe-inspiring thought. If men found that they could produce supermen at will, what would the

[1] *Behaviorism.*
[2] *Psychological Care of Infant and Child.*

supermen afterwards do with their creators, and would they necessarily approve of their own propagation? Or if we chose rather a world of cultured gentlemen, what might they think of our experiments on babies?

However, as this account of genius ieaves out infant prodigies, who seem particularly to require explanation from the Behaviorist standpoint, perhaps we need not yer take the proposition too seriouslv. Ordinary observation (which is almost all we have at present in these fields) tells us that habit is not, in fact, the all-powerful master of human conduct that Behaviorism suggests. It is strong enough, certainly, but probably most people have come across at least one case of sudden, violent change of habits, if not one of the surprising multiple personality cases recorded by psychiatrists.

One wonders, for example, how

Watson would explain the elderly lady who, after a life of exemplary Victorian altruism, was converted in the course of a slight illness to the view that it was time her neighbours had their share of the blessing of self-sacrifice; and behaved accordingly for the rest of her life. There is also religious conversion and other types. As to cases of loss of memory, it is difficult to see how behavioristic theory could cover them at all except by presuming always some extremely complicated physical injury.

If Dr Watson is ever confronted with these problems, no doubt he promptly reacts with formulæ which include them, just as Freud threw out wing after wing of the Preconscious and the Percept-Conscious and the Super-Ego in that wonderful Gothic structure, with gargoyles complete, *The Ego and the Id.* This elasticity is, in fact, one of the most disconcerting properties of psychological theories. Their capacity for explanatoriness, like that of Medieval Christianity, seems to be unlimited. Hypotheses in other sciences are verified or refuted by the fulfilment or failure of their predictions. The theory of Relativity would have had short shrift if the position of the stars at the eclipse had not corresponded to Einstein's calculations. But when Watson finds that some human beings do not behave as expected, or Freud comes across cases that (as he says) "get worse during the treatment instead of getting better," the theory is merely let out a little here, or drawn in a little there to take in the rebellious phenomena, until it has lost all shapeliness and intelligibility.

One is driven once more to the conclusion that this cussed human nature of ours is singularly unamenable to scientific method. Some perverse factor comes in, where and when exactly it is impossible to say. Sisyphus pushes his stone up and up the hill, from inorganic matter to organic, from unicellular life to multicellular, through plant, invertebrate, fish, amphibian, reptile, bird, mammal. We may know exactly what our dog is capable of, and what to expect of him. Even the human infant is, to all appearance, a little animal and nothing more; or, at least, there are parents—even mothers—found to say that their babies fulfil Dr Watson's formulæ precisely. And some people never grow up at all, so that it is possible to discover approximately their "mental ages" and to deal with them more or less according to rule—though even dogs and morons may surprise one occasionally. But the experimenter pushes further and further and comes to individuals who, for instance, (as Watson says) "do not readily show conditioned reflexes." In other words, he has begun to meet his equals, who not only may not produce the reaction he expects, but may even turn round and begin to ask awkward questions about his own reactions—on what principles he arranges his experiments, what directs his choice of subjects, whether there are any personal peculiarities in his interpretation of his results. They might, for example, wish to retrace the sources of that insistence on the mischievous effects of parental fondness, which seems to be as much Dr Watson's King Charles's head as the sex instinct is Freud's. It seems pertinent to inquire of Dr Watson why we should attach any absolute value to the reactions of a self-confessed robot? Sometimes he seems himself vaguely aware of the threatening paradox. There is a peculiar intellectual naïveté in the writing of a book full of logical reasoning and addressed, as a scientific work must be, to that abstraction, the impartial intellect, and then confessing at its conclusion that the author is trying "to dangle a stimulus in front of you, a verbal stimulus which, if acted upon, will gradually change this universe."[1] Most people think the universe might well be changed in some respects, but we need a more convincing reason than this for trying to do it.

[1] *Behaviorism.*

IV

"To change the world" . . . On such sketchy foundations, and in spite of its own constant protestations of scientific detachment, Behaviorism has, in fact, already developed its ideal of human nature. This seems to be a tendency so persistent in psychological theory, that one is driven to wonder whether it is not an inevitable phase of it—whether it is, in fact, possible for man to investigate his own nature without becoming moral and didactic about it. No other science develops ideals in this way. Applied mathematics, applied physics offer to show man how to get what he wants in their particular spheres when he has already decided what it is that he wants—whether a building, or an aeroplane, or an anæsthetic, or a poison gas. Only Psychology insists on telling him, in the first place, what he ought to want.

The figure shining through the mists at the top of the hill up which the Behaviorist labours with his stone is very unlike that impressive classical statue of the psycho-analysts—"The Primacy of the Intelligence." It seems to be made of plasticine, rather than of marble. It is that of the perfectly adapted man.

"The old argument," says Watson, "that a good many millions of children have been successfully reared in the past few million years has just about broken down in the light of the now generally recognized lack of success of most people in making satisfactory adjustments to society."[1] And (*à propos* of agitators) "The behaviorist would like to develop his world of people from

[1] *Psychology from the Standpoint of a Behaviorist.*

birth on, so that their speech and their bodily behaviour could equally well be exhibited freely everywhere without running foul of group standards.'"[1]

And when this is done, no doubt the human race can rest, for there will obviously be no reason why it should go any further. If that extremely well-planned institution, the Feudal System, had been applied to men who had fitted into it like parts of a machine, is there any reason why we should not still have been living under it? One doubts if Dr Watson would approve of that result, even though, if it had so happened, we should, in the nature of the case, be convinced that we were living in the best of all possible worlds and be perfectly satisfied. But if, as matters now are, we were to let him bring up the next generation on this principle of maximum adaptation, would it turn out to be a generation of

[1] *Behaviorism.*

geniuses, or of cultured gentlemen, or of standardized Henry Fords? In the last event, we might wish to consider the proposal a little in the first place, and even give a thought as to our own fitness, ill-adapted and poorly-functioning mechanisms as we are, to choose the lines on which future generations are to be developed.

It is chastening to reflect that the persons we most admire in past ages were often just those who were, in their own day, least at home in the world. Shelley, for instance, who walked with the unconscious nakedness of Eden into an assembled company, would have fared as badly in a Behaviorist laboratory as the author of *Songs of Innocence* in a psycho-analyst's consulting-room. The founder of Christianity was so ill-adapted that he got himself executed as a common criminal; yet our society as we know it, including New York and Dr Watson, could hardly have existed if he had not. On the other hand, as Jung pointed out, an individual well adjusted to a mistaken society may very well perish with it.

Dr Watson is too sound a thinker to be able to be consistent about this business of adaptation, which like most psychological problems, becomes more involved the more one thinks about it. At times he identifies his ideal, adapted man with the man that society wants, and declares that his job, like that of other workers in applied science, is to produce what is ordered. But it is not so easy to decide what society wants. Is the bootlegger wanted or not in the United States, for instance? Is the society which decides what is wanted to be local society, the society of a town, or a class, or a country, or of the great world? A man who fails in Tennessee may thrive in Vienna. The man most successful in a country at peace may not remain equally successful if his country goes to war. Even in the narrower sphere of politics, a jingo statesman, triumphant at home, may find himself a misfit at Geneva. In the same way, a young American of the commercial classes, who regards an insult as a sportsman regards a knock and goes on as if nothing had happened, will not find the habit adds to his prestige if his firm sends him to France.

If it were adaptability rather than adaptedness that were in question, the ideal would be more understandable, if not more attractive. But there is no room for such an abstraction in the Behaviorist system. A man either is, or is not, trained to behave in such and such ways in such and such situations; in a new situation, he can only fall back on rat-in-the-maze behaviour. Thus, unless the precise course of a child's life could be mapped out at birth, it is hard to see how he could be trained to meet it. Roughly speaking, one may say that such types are acceptable in such places, but hardly with the precision necessary for scientific manufacture. On the moral side indeed, most of us do at least agree that standards should be uniform, and we might perhaps begin sending in our designs for ideal adapted man; but it still remains to decide who is to judge the competition.

Dr Watson would not perhaps refuse the office, if it were offered to him. For he does not really want to produce the human being that existing society might specify, if it were capable of specifying anything clearly. Like everyone else who thinks at all, he sees many cases where he would prefer to adapt the environment to the individual rather than the individual to the environment. He will certainly have run foul of some group standards in his excursion into ethics:

"Sometime we will have a behaviorist ethics, experimental in type, which will tell us whether it is advisable from the standpoint of present and future adjustments of the individual to have one wife or many wives; to have capital punishment or punishment of any kind; whether prohibition or no prohibition, easy divorces or no divorces, whether many of our prescribed courses of conduct make for the adjustment of the individual or the contrary, such, for example, as having a family life, or not even knowing our own fathers and mothers."[1]

It would be difficult to find a passage more unconsciously paradoxical. If the individual is not to be adjusted to follow these "prescribed courses of conduct," how is he to be adjusted? It is precisely these—"the body and speech habits that society demands" that Watson has offered to produce.

Appeal is here clearly to another

[1] *Behaviorism.*

authority—to what Dr Watson thinks society ought to demand—what he thinks would be good for it. And, with this, one is at liberty to agree or not. But with the term "experimental ethics" everyone must quarrel. For it implies an ethical principle already established—that conduct is to be judged by its consequences. Incidentally, it is a short step from this to "the end justifies the means," and this unproved premise seems to be at the base of at least some of the behaviour of the Behaviorists.

V

A SOCIETY of Henry Fords would not really do, even from the most advanced Behaviorist's standpoint. After all, if we were all Henry Fords, our environment would be so altered that we should no longer be adapted to it. The successful 'old boy,' coming to speak at a prize-giving, tells his young friends how they may go and do likewise, while everyone happily forgets that he is addressing at most two or three of his audience, since the obscurity of the many is the condition of the prominence of the one.

"When everyone is somebody,
Then no one's anybody."

SISYPHUS

If Dr Watson and his colleagues had charge of the younger generation, they would have to bring up some to direct and some to obey, some to work with their hands and some with their larynxes, and with infinitely finer and more complicated variations than these. But most practical psychologists admit inborn differences in mental make-up, and thus put far from themselves the fateful decisions that the Behaviorist is so cheerfully ready to make, even as bees decide (though on what principles no one yet knows), which grubs shall be queens and which workers.

Nevertheless, given your people, it is, in a limited sense, to everyone's interest that they should be as well adapted as possible to their particular position in life. More especially is it to the interest of those who are already well satisfied with the existing state of society. This fact, no doubt, accounts for the present haste to apply this youngest of the sciences in industry and business at a time when scientists in other fields will still hardly admit its right to be called a science at all. As a natural consequence, psychological methods in industry seem to be peculiarly of the hit-or-miss type. Failing firm leads from their colleagues in the laboratories, the practical men have to do their experimenting as they go along. It is again a question of the rat in the maze, dashing wildly about, trying one way after another, and not of the ape sitting down quietly to think the matter out. And again, the interested layman may find more than one suggestion that out of this particular maze, there is in fact, no ultimate exit. Or, to go back to our original metaphor, Sisyphus seems to find that the substitution of a log for a stone does not really help him to the top of the hill.

SISYPHUS

As might be expected, the outstanding triumphs of the industrial psychologist are chiefly on the physiological side. Many workers who struggled on, working in a bad light, or in cramped postures, or with insufficient or badly timed rest pauses have reason to be grateful to him. The difficulty begins further on. It was natural to pass from the obvious easing of physical and nervous friction to an ideal 'one best way' of working—that is, the position, movements and speed for the workmen in any process of labour which could be shown to produce maximum results. Yet it seems that this 'one best way' is not, in fact, always the best way, because the workmen object to it. In a survey recently published by the staff of the National Institute of Industrial Psychology, the practice is criticized from the inside:

" This phrase is an excellent slogan and appeals to a certain type of manager, but unfortunately it does not agree with ascertained physiological and psychological facts. The musculature of no two persons is identical and on the mental side there is equal divergence . . . . High production can be and has been forced in this way, but at too great a cost. . . . The psychological effect of restriction of a worker's activities is still not sufficiently realized. There is in all animals—and the human species is no exception—a tendency to resist limitations of activity."

The writer goes on to allude to Pavlov's observations on that dog which so surprised his scientific innocence by its violent objection to being (quite loosely and comfortably) fastened by the legs, and his consequent postulation of a special 'freedom reflex' in animals. Watson would, no doubt, identify this 'reflex' with the ' rage reaction ' aroused in infants (and, according to his observations, in no other way) by the physical restraint of their movements.

This 'freedom reflex,' by whatever name one calls it, has possibly an importance for practical psychologists greater than they have yet surmised. It might have even a fatal importance.

Our psychologist, however, goes on to point out that more can be done towards increasing production (and he is a man of business; to increase production is, after all, his main point) by the action of more remote incentives than by the enforcing of the ' one best way.' In other words, just as one can get an animal to go through fantastic antics by the promise of food or the fear of the whip, so men can be induced to work at high pressure by the attraction of high wages and the fear of dismissal.

This possibility has also, of course,

its limits. It is common gossip in the United States that only the strongest men in the prime of life can stand the strain of Ford standard production, and that even they can stand it only for a very short time:

> " We worked eleven hours a day," says Robert Cruden of the Packard Works at Detroit.[1] " After five in the afternoon we would get up on the cross beams and work away in a semi-conscious state, putting out in two hours half as much as we usually put out in an hour. . . . One night I actually went to sleep leaning against a body and was saved from the wrath of the boss only by a worker, who gave me a push. We usually left the plant around seven at night, most of us too tired to run to the street-car. I left home at six in the morning and returned at eight, ill-tempered and on edge. I

[1] In the New York *Nation*, June 12th, 1929, " No Loitering, Get out Production."

would eat whatever was set before me, sullenly and without question and then collapse into bed. There I would lie until wakened at 5.30 the next morning. Working, eating and sleeping were my sole functions."

Common report has it that men who can stand the strain put in a year or two in these Detroit high speed factories, earning large sums, and then stagger away to months of blissful idleness and free spending elsewhere; so that Detroit has become the centre of a rapidly shifting population, using the rest of the country as its dust-bin. Such reports and rumours seem to cast a doubt on the much canvassed possibility of applying Ford methods to industry in general.

The pressure exerted here is indirect as against the direct enforcement of the 'one best way,' but Mr Cruden's article shows clearly enough that, in the long run, it calls out the 'rage reaction' no less vigorously. He reports that the grumbling in the Detroit factory would have "gladdened the heart of an agitator," and that the workers there are eagerly awaiting the fulfilment of the Federation of Labour's promise to organize the automobile industry.

There are other indirect methods for getting 'the best' out of industrial workers. British Trade Unions have done much to check the happy thought of ranging the workers in competing groups. More success attends efforts to stimulate the 'team spirit' in factories and offices. Let the employees have clubs, sports, magazines and other sociabilities in common and it is to be expected that they will develop *esprit de corps,* work better together and produce more profitable results. These methods have been applied in England in recent years to an unprecedented degree; how far they have, in fact, done away with the worker's sense of being exploited, of being regarded as 'food for factories,' strike records and the spread of Socialism may be taken to indicate.

The practical psychologist's power of handling men seems, in short, to be limited by this objection that men have to being handled. The cunning practitioner may, for some time, succeed in handling them without letting them know that he is doing so. Dr Little, an American expert, tells of a firm that is doing well by selecting its workers for stupidity. But all workers cannot be morons; and, in dealing with men, the psychologist again comes up against his own humanity.

There is an amusing discussion of the 'interview' in the symposium of the Institute of Industrial Psychology already quoted. It is candidly admitted that tests of skill and intelligence will never be a complete substitute for this trying function in the selection of candidates for a position. Care must first be taken to put the applicant at his ease. (Those who have played the part of victim on these occasions know the frightfulness of that process). The employer then proceeds on standard lines with the questions most likely to evoke replies revealing the presence or absence of those abilities which were found by analysis to be requisite, listed and marked under heads A, B, C, D, etc. It sounds efficient and, no doubt, is so up to a point. But the writer, with saving common sense, also recognizes that "the interview is still so dependent on the interaction between two personalities that it is extremely difficult to eliminate all extraneous prejudices. The interviewer himself, being a living person, cannot possibly be the same at all times. Anyone who has done much interviewing knows that he is in a very different condition of affability when interviewing the fifteenth candidate than when he was interviewing the first. And an applicant coming after a good candidate may have quite a different reception from that he would have received if he had come after a poor one."

It is the same stumbling-block—that the investigator is made of the same stuff as the investigated. He must keep himself in hand to a degree hardly possible to a normal human being; and, after that, he must discount the effects of the strain of keeping himself in hand. It is even conceivable that the applicant also may know something of Psychology, and may be using his knowledge.

This odd game of hide-and-seek which develops as soon as practical psychology tries to go beyond the more superficial aspects of human personality finds humorous illustration in the great new industry of advertising. The case seems to be similar to the race between the offensive and the defensive weapon in warfare. In time the public becomes immune to certain modes of attack and new ones must be invented. The one in vogue in New York in 1928 was expressly classified as the "Appeal to Fear" technique. Placards announcing that "no one is safe from body-odour" and warnings of like nature met the eye at every turn. How far such methods proved successful the layman has no means of knowing. One may conjecture, however, that they would not continue to be successful long. Apart from the increasing minority which is becoming contra-suggestible to advertisement, and is hardly likely to be conciliated by this form of blackmail, the technique had become a standing joke. "No one will want to know you, if you don't use

Redoleo." The corresponding 'aggressive' tactics in salesmen quickly defeat their own ends in the same manner. People see advertisements in the newspapers asking for agents with "intelligence, loyalty, aggressiveness, and vision," smile, and are prepared for the ingenuously browbeating youngsters of both sexes who carry on a perpetual siege of New York flats. Nor do the more soothing forms of salesmanship often win a more lasting victory. "I simply daren't go into that shop now," people say, "he's too good a salesman," and turn away in thankfulness to the cheap take-it-or-leave-it stores where the manner of the assistants is official, if not actually forbidding. And the stores abound, flourish, and multiply.

If some big agency would publish audited statistics to show how the results of the old method of physical reiteration in advertisement compare in the long run with those of the ingenious type now used, it is possible that much time and money might be saved. Perhaps our advertisers and salesmen are still far enough ahead of their public to get good value for their threats, expostulations, lectures, jokes, exhortations, all working round to the use of So-and-so's cocoa, or face-cream, or motor fuel, or stockings. But we seem to be rapidly approaching a stage when, both in advertisement and in the less obviously venal forms of journalism, no one not certifiably feeble-minded will believe a word that he sees printed. Perhaps there will presently come a point when the best technique will be to depreciate the goods one wants to sell. One firm already announces its fabrics with the headline "not recommended for durability." But even this will not avail indefinitely.

In short, the advertiser, like other

psychologists, needs to be superhuman. His fellow human beings will always have a possible surprise in reserve for the merely human one.

THE LIMITS OF PSYCHOLOGY

VI

ONE of the most alarming of Mr H. G. Wells's fantasies described the descent upon the world of a race developed far beyond it in the smaller and older planet of Mars. These creatures, with bodies sacrificed to their brains, regarded human beings as inferior animals to be either used for food or destroyed by heat-rays and poison gases. If, on the other hand, they had seen in man a potential useful slave and had taken the trouble to study his workings, physical and mental, they might be imagined to succeed in the task to which our mere earthly psychologists will probably always be inadequate. Being outside humanity, they would have been able to get a clear view of it, a feat impossible to our boldest geniuses who, like the philosopher-poet himself who created the idea of the super-man, have always been 'human, all-too-human.' Their own weaknesses intrude, and since the mind of man is an integration or nothing, and cannot be understood in fragments, these weaknesses are liable to mar the whole fabric of their thought.

Fortunately, there is more than one type of knowledge, and our understanding of human nature is not confined to what scientists can tell us. "You can either ride it, or you can overhaul it; but you can't do both," said some humorist when the bicycle was the latest new thing. It would be cynically unfair to the best psychologists to press the comparison to the extreme, but, at least, if we have to remain incompletely analysed, we can still go on living and thinking. After all, mind, like the bicycle, is made for action, and it seems possible that it can come nearest to understanding itself in action—whether in life, or, more freely and typically, in art.

Even among psychiatrists, the most successful often seem to work on artistic lines rather than on scientific. It is a common gibe that those best able to help fellow human beings in mental or nervous troubles are often people of high-strung temperament, who hold in check by will and intelligence a potential instability in themselves—but sometimes, of course, lose the battle, since they take heavy risks. Such physicians work less by rule than by intuition, and the gibes thus seem to be misplaced, for their own hypersensitiveness is probably the measure of their capacity to understand and assist others. Formulæ about the human mind are as little to the point in such cases as they were to Dostoieffsky, the epileptic, who passed beyond the psycho-analysts long before Psycho-analysis had been heard of.

In this sense, the great writers are the master-workers in Psychology. It would be a rash psychologist who would be prepared to say that he understood more of human nature than did Shakespeare or Goethe or Dostoieffsky. Theirs is, of course, understanding of a different type, but perhaps more proper to its subject matter. And the reader, or watcher, or listener, learns by participation rather than by intellectual analysis, in the same way that the feeling in one's muscles as one watches a bird, tells one something more satisfying about flight than does the laboratory dissection of a wing.

Volumes have been written as to whether Hamlet was mad or not. If Hamlet were here now, it might be necessary to decide the question in a practical manner. (An alienist has, in fact, recently written a volume to explain that he would have certified all Shakespeare's tragic characters.) But, as it is, the question seems about as important as the older one—how many angels could dance upon the point of a needle. No one, I believe, has ever raised any question whether or not Hamlet is true to life. We understand him as we watch, or read, the play without knowing in the least whether he is mad or not, or what madness is, or whether it is definable. I have heard Hamlet's character explained by a man of science as a case of 'repressed ambition,' but I doubt if anyone of average sensibility will find the explanation illuminating, or any explanation required.

Characters like Hamlet are in the broad highway of life. It seems that almost everyone (whether certifiable or not) has in him a potential Hamlet, just as he has a potential Faust, a Bovary, a Soames Forsyte, a Peter Pan, even a potential Christ. These are characters of the type that E. M. Forster describes as done 'in the round,' contrasting them with the Gamps and Micawbers done 'in the flat.' One may carry the distinction a stage further back, and suspect that 'round' characters are those experienced from the inside, possible and incipient personalities of their creator, as also of most of his readers. They express traits and tendencies that the scientific psychologist has to take into account in his generalizations about human nature.

Other 'round' characters begin where the psychologist's generalizations begin to fail. If one must have mental tests, it would not be a bad one to find out which among these 'round' characters, created by masters, the tested person was capable of appreciating. An important one would be Nikolay Stavrogin in *The Possessed,* the readers of which seem to be sharply divided into those who find him quite unintelligible, and those who are fascinated almost to the point of obsession and cannot imagine why he needs any more explanation than Hamlet.

In this character, Dostoieffsky, in fact, approaches the baffling central mystery of the human mind—the rounding of consciousness upon itself. Nikolay is the man who watches himself at a double remove—not the mere self-dramatist like Madame Bovary, nor the mere self-critic like Hamlet, but another more remote cynical and deadly consciousness which itself watches the dramatist and the critic. Stultified thus, it is impossible for him to take himself seriously, or, in consequence, to take anything else seriously. He is incapable even of the effort by which the ' introvert ' sometimes transforms himself into an ' extravert ' by clutching with deliberately blind obstinacy at some "As if" philosophy –that tendency which perhaps accounts for the fact that, where brilliant men are not agnostics, they are frequently Roman Catholics; since, if one must accept some working hypothesis, the more complete and definite it is the better. But such a self-limitation is impossible to Stavrogin, though he tries spasmodically to give his world meaning by desperate perversities of conduct. Meanwhile, his distinction of personality fascinates everyone who meets him, so that they, at least, take him seriously and make him the centre of their ideals and ambitions, from the bustling revolutionary who sees him as Ivan the Tsarevitch, redeemer of Russia, to Darya Pavlovna, who merely wishes to mother him. In turn, he disappoints them all, seeing what he is doing and unable to care.

It is a dramatic fantasia on that achievement of consciousness in man which makes him unique among animals, and which remains the free, dangerous, intractable element in human nature, rendering it impossible to treat men as machines and liable to falsify all the predictions of psychologists. A psycho-analyst would have been at a loss with Nikolay Stavrogin, for there would have been nothing for him to bring to consciousness. The trouble was in the other direction. But smaller personalities may be equally baffling by grace of this faculty which has no master in the known universe. To take a crude instance, a man may lose his temper like an animal because he is provoked. He may, on the other hand, restrain it by exercising self-control. It may, on the contrary, occur to him to restrain it and he may decide that it is not worth his while or that to show anger may serve his purpose. The possible twists in the maze of consciousness are endless and no psychologist is ever likely to find his way through them, however many trials and errors he may make. He may try to escape it, like Watson, by denying its existence, but few have the courage, or the blindness, for that counsel of despair. Yet the mere attempt to approach the problem directly brings a curious sense of weariness and repulsion—the intuition of futility. It is only the artist, edging towards the mystery, darting from tree to tree, catching glimpses instantly lost again, who can begin to show us something of our own uniqueness.

Dostoieffsky's is perhaps the most nearly direct assault ever made, or likely to be made, on this citadel of human nature; but more cunning artists have other modes of approach.

Pirandello deepens and exercises the subjective faculty by his tricks of technique. He places the audience itself, by means of plays within plays, by dual personalities and other devices, at the further remove from the outside world. It is an unwonted discipline which irritates many play-goers to the point of exasperation. His less sophisticated enemies dismiss the dramatist as 'high-brow'; the more sophisticated ones call him a charlatan. Pirandello himself rejoices in all his critics in a play devoted to them, well aware that only something vital makes people as angry as all that.

Pirandello's method seems, none the less, dangerously near the edge of what is possible in this direction. The more typical imaginative writer, looking inward, naturally uses symbolism. Even Dostoieffsky calls up demons and doubles for Stavrogin and Ivan Karamazov, though these appallingly lucid individuals are always well aware that any phantoms they may see are their own hallucinations, and have no outside existence. It is only a step from this to the dramatization of the powers and aspects of the mind such as were common in medieval poetry and drama.

It seems doubtful whether Freud would be flattered to be called a spoilt artist. But if his system had been cast as a romance or a fantastic play, it might have been interesting, moving, perhaps even beautiful. It would also have been harmless, since no one would have tried to act upon it literally. The psycho-analytic version of human nature is intensely dramatic, with its imprisoned complexes, its rebellious Libido, its stern Censor, its bewildered and frustrated Ego. It is a construction comparable to Bunyan's *Holy War*, in which King Shaddai and Prince Diabolus fight for the town of Man-soul, with its Mayor, Understanding, and its Recorder, Conscience. Probably its relation to truth is similar in kind.

This dramatic quality has certainly been one factor in the popularity of Freudian theory. Another has been the literary quality of Freud's books, most of which are readable to a degree rare in scientific writings. There is poetic imagination even in many of the phrases:

"Now when a child grows up and finds that he is destined to remain a child for ever and that he can never do without protection against unknown and mighty powers. . . ."[1]

"The normal man is not only far more immoral than he believes, but also far more moral than he has any idea of."[2]

Freud has even analysed a romance,

[1] *The Future of an illusion.*
[2] *The Ego and the Id.*

not, as do many of his disciples, in the hope of discovering the personality of the author, but allegorizing in his own terms the story of the characters itself —an odd enterprise for a scientist. If he were ever to undertake an imaginative work, which is not, after all, so great a step from creative criticism, literature might be enriched from an unexpected source.

But whether a Shakespeare, a Pirandello, or a Freud, the artist gives one man's experience, and those for whom it has meaning recognize and share it. Apart from accidents of technical skill, the greater the capacity for experience, the greater the artist. He is what one might call an ' inclusive ' man, like the successful psychological healer, and can help others because, in the literal sense of the word, he comprehends them, as the whole contains the part. If he uses artistic form, that gives him a subtler power of qualification which becomes more important in painting and sculpture, and especially in music, than in literature. Many people were given a new conception of Jesus by looking at Epstein's statue, receiving it not only from the austerity of the face and attitude, but from the composition as a whole. The experience expressed in a Beethoven sonata can only be inadequately interpreted in words by means of a distant symbolism by those capable of receiving it.

This element in art makes of it something fundamentally other than science. In a passage in *The Strange Necessity,* Rebecca West seems to take literature as a kind of advanced Behaviorism where, since the experiments cannot be performed on men, they are performed on dummies of the imagination. She believes the feelings of satisfaction or dissatisfaction with which a man reads a novel or a poem representing human beings enacting life "is due to a conviction that the representation of it is or is not parallel to what occurs in real life" and compares them to his feeling "when shown a drawing of a human figure that is or is not 'out of drawing.'" If this were the whole truth, we should have to regard art as little more than a slipshod form of science. But it hardly covers the fact that the most impressive paintings and statues often show figures to make an anatomical expert tear his hair, that Browning and Henry James make their characters say things that no human being could conceivably utter; that David Garnett's lovely fantasy turns on an episode that (as in the Frenchman's final criticism) is "*physiologiquement impossible*"; music can hardly be brought under it.

The artist's comment on his facts—often an emotional rather than a rational comment—may be more vital than the facts themselves. The action of his own mind and not merely the activities he displays is the source of æsthetic satisfaction. He makes a strength of what is the scientist's weakness—his own individuality. His appreciators are those who feel, or can be brought to feel, about his subject matter as he himself felt about it. And the fact of their so feeling is the important one in an æsthetic experience. The nature of the enlightenment given by art seems to be not specifically intellectual understanding (though that may be present), but that sense of spiritual purification which, in its most poignant form, in tragedy, Aristotle called "*katharsis*," showing that even the master-systematizer could not put it into logical terms. Mind, rejoicing in its own activity, finds that the devastating figure of Nikolay Stavrogin is not only comprehensible, but is a fine thing, and that it is magnificent that he should exist; and that Pirandello's self-torturers are, after all, the least futile of created beings.

THE LIMITS OF PSYCHOLOGY

VII

MEANWHILE Sisyphus continues undauntedly to labour up the hill and Münchausen to tug hopefully at his queue. Yet many even among the scientists are not quite comfortable about this youngest of the sciences.

J. B. S. Haldane, who may, perhaps, if anyone, be taken as typical of the modern scientific outlook, does not believe that Psychology can at present rank as a science, though he thinks that it will so rank some day, when Physiology and Chemistry have sufficiently prepared the way.[1] To him, it is merely a question of increasing complexity and not of any impracticability in the subject matter. It would be helpful if

[1] In *Possible Worlds*.

he, or some other, equipped for the work, would consider also the question whether our psychological theorists are not only trying to go further than their present knowledge warrants, but further than knowledge ever can warrant.

Such an abstruse question might be supposed hardly to concern the unscientific outsider, who is apt to feel as he looks at the theses of the various psychological schools, like the jury at the trial of the Knave of Hearts, quite uncertain whether the word should be "important" or "unimportant." It is just this point that Psychology can be, and is, so summarily applied to life that gives the matter at least a local urgency. Our bright young people come along, asking, like the graduate of the Lohengrin University, Texas, in Edith Wharton's novel *The Children,* "Can you give me, for instance, any sort of assurance that Astorre and

Beatrice have ever been properly psycho-analysed and that their studies and games have been selected with a view to their particular moral, alimentary, dental, and glandular heredity? Games, for instance, should be quite as carefully supervised as studies. . ." Some of us who, in the Dark Ages, selected our own games (and bloodthirsty enough they were, too, sometimes) still feel a little sympathy for Astorre and Beatrice, and would like to be sure that, if they must suffer, it is not in a cause that will be forgotten to-morrow.

The verdict, since we cannot decide for ourselves, seems to be: 'Wanted—a Philosopher'—one who will mark out the bounds of Psychology, as Kant marked out those of Metaphysics, when he made it unnecessary to speculate any further about such problems as those of Infinity, the First Cause and others to which human reason is inapplicable, but on which so much ingenuity had before his time been expended.

As one glances over the labours of psychologists and notes their difficulties and contradictions, it becomes impossible not to suspect that the Nature of Consciousness may be found to be thus outside the bounds. And, with it, might possibly be carried that question of the freedom of choice, which so exercises the minds of most children, as well as those of adults of the kind that never quite grow up, but become instead artists, scientists or philosophers. Can I choose what I will do, or not? Is my very choice predetermined by my moral, alimentary, dental, and glandular heredity, or (if one prefers Watson's view) by my upbringing? If it could ever be shown conclusively that this problem was scientifically irrelevant, we might get on better with the soluble problems. Whether, again, the definition of the ideal man would still be found remaining among these soluble problems is another point for our philosopher to determine. And, in doing this, he would decide whether there could ever be such a thing as a science of morals.

Nor would this process be a mere physical amputation of so much area cut off from what can be definitely known. Its removal would modify the remaining dominions of Psychology, as ceded territory alters the whole economy of a state. If it implied less certainty, less inducement to try to cut to pattern the minds and lives of other people than some psychologists show at present, this might not be a serious loss. It is pleasant and satisfactory to know, but merely to think one knows is apt to lead to less happy results. Science has, in general, the air of becoming less and less nearly exact as it mounts higher. When it reaches man's higher faculties, there may be found to be a debatable ground where intellect gradually gives place to action as the only available means to understanding.

Printed in Great Britain by
MACKAYS LTD., CHATHAM.

For Product Safety Concerns and Information please contact our EU representative GPSR@taylorandfrancis.com Taylor & Francis Verlag GmbH, Kaufingerstraße 24, 80331 München, Germany